Plant
Reproduction

Barbara Somervill

www.raintreepublishers.co.uk
Visit our website to find out more information about Raintree books.

To order:

☎ Phone +44 (0) 1865 888066

▤ Fax +44 (0) 1865 314091

▣ Visit www.raintreepublishers.co.uk

Raintree is an imprint of Capstone Global Library Limited, a company incorporated in England and Wales having its registered office at 7 Pilgrim Street, London, EC4V 6LB – Registered company number: 6695582

"Raintree" is a registered trademark of Pearson Education Limited, under licence to Capstone Global Library Limited

Text © Capstone Global Library Limited 2009
First published in hardback in 2009
Paperback edition first published in 2010
The moral rights of the proprietor have been asserted.

Edited by Megan Cotugno and Andrew Farrow
Designed by Philippa Jenkins
Original illustrations ©Pearson Education Ltd
Illustrated by KJA-artists.com
Picture research by Ruth Blair
Originated by Modern Age Repro House Ltd
Printed and bound in China by Leo Paper Products Ltd

ISBN 978 1 406210 53 8 (hardback)
13 12 11 10 09
10 9 8 7 6 5 4 3 2 1

ISBN 978 1 406210 62 0 (paperback)
14 13 12 11 10
10 9 8 7 6 5 4 3 2 1

British Library Cataloguing in Publication Data
Somervill, Barbara A.
Plant reproduction. - (Sci-hi)
571.8'2
A full catalogue record for this book is available from the British Library.

Acknowledgements
We would like to thank the following for allowing their pictures to be reproduced in this publication: © Alamy/ www.white-windmill.co.uk p. **40**; © Getty Images/Time & Life Pictures p. **27**; © Corbis/Scott T. Smith p. **31**; © iStockphoto/Klaudia Steiner p. **31**; © naturepl.com/ Adrian Davis p. **38**; ©naturepl.com/Jose B. Ruiz p. **19**; © naturepl.com/Jurgen Freund pp. **20/21**; © Pearson Education Ltd/Debbie Rowe p. **28**; © Pearson Education Ltd/Philippa Jenkins pp. **iii** (Contents), **23**, **26**, **29**, **30**, **32**, **33**, **37**; © Photodisc pp. **title page**, **25**; © Photodisc/StockTrek p. **18**; © Photolibrary Group/ Botanica pp. **4/5**, **36**; © Photolibrary Group/Japan Travel Bureau p. **24**; © Photolibrary Group/Robert Palomba p. **8**; © Science Photo Library/Andrew Brown p. **35**; © Science Photo Library/Archie Young p. **29**; © Science Photo Library/James H. Robinson p. **iii** (Contents), **14**; © Shutterstock pp. **42/43**, background images and design features throughout; © Shutterstock/ Marie C. Fields pp. **12/13**.

Cover photographs reproduced with permission of © Naturepl/Premaphotos main; © Naturepl/Bernard Castelein inset

The publishers would like to thank literacy consultant Nancy Harris and content consultant Casey Rand for their assistance in the preparation of this book.

Every effort has been made to contact copyright holders of any material reproduced in this book. Any omissions will be rectified in subsequent printings if notice is given to the publishers.

Some words are shown in bold, like this. These words are explained in the glossary. You will find important information and definitions underlined, like this.

Contents

Why do we have bees like this one to thank for most of the fruit and vegetables we eat? Find out on page 14

How did a Peruvian plant called SOLANUM TUBEROSA become the ancestor of 200 species of potatoes? See page 26

What is a plant?

Our lives depend on plants. Green plants, such as grass, trees, and green **algae**, clean the air we breathe. Almost all the foods we eat are either plants, seeds of plants, or products from animals that feed on plants.

A plant is a living **organism** that makes its own food. Plants have life cycles that include a form of birth, growth, and **reproduction.** There are about 350,000 different green plant species. The majority of those plants (over 250,000) are flowering plants. These numbers do not include fungi, such as mushrooms and toadstools. **Lichens**, which are a blend of fungi and algae, are also not included.

Ferns are plants that produce spores, not seeds. One fern can produce 3,000,000 spores.

Land plants

Some plant species can grow in water. However, most plant species grow on land. Land plants are divided into two basic groups: **vascular** plants and **non-vascular** plants. A vascular plant has special tissues that move water and food through the plant. Common vascular plants are trees, fruits, vegetables, and flowers. Non-vascular plants do not have tissues for moving food and water through the plant. They include peat moss, sphagnum moss, liverworts, and hornworts.

Land plant groups	Divisions	Examples
Vascular plants	Seed-producing plants without flowers	Pines, gingkos, banksias, firs
	Seed-producing plants with flowers	Oaks, elms, roses, lilies, broccoli, cabbage, apples, berries
	Seedless plants	Ferns, horsetails, club mosses
Non-vascular plants		True mosses, liverworts, hornworts

The earliest plants

The earliest plants lived in the oceans. Some fossils of these early plants date back more than 3 billion years. Plants still fill oceans, seas, rivers, and streams with life. The slime that coats your fish tank is algae, the same plant that thrives in all clean water environments. Algae and other water plants provide food for thousands of creatures. They put oxygen into the water and filter out pollution. Marine plants provide nurseries for baby fish to grow.

Parts of a plant

There are many different types of plants. However, plants have the same parts.

Stems, which carry water and food from the roots to a plant's leaves, also provide a support system for the plant.

Roots are important, because they absorb **nutrients**, as well as water, from the soil.

Leaves are one of the defining characteristics of a plant, and the **cuticle** serves as their outer layer. It helps protect against **bacteria**.

Finally, for flowering plants, flowers are the key reproductive parts of a plant.

Study the diagram and learn even more about the parts of a plant!

FLOWERS

Flowers are the reproductive organs of flowering plants. Flowers make seeds, which allow parent plants to produce young plants. Without flowers, we would have no vegetables, fruits, nuts, or grains.

LEAVES

Plants make food in their leaves. Leaves can come in many shapes and sizes, from tiny blades of grass to the broad leaves of the elephant plant. Some plants (for example oaks and roses) have single leaves. Other plants (ashes and locusts) have compound leaves with many small leaflets.

STEM
Stems carry water and food from the roots to the leaves and flower. They support the upper part of the plant so that the leaves can receive sunlight.

ROOTS
Roots take in water and nutrients from the soil. Some roots can be eaten, such as carrots and parsnips.

CUTICLE
The cuticle is the waxy covering on most plants that protects the leaves and stems from drying out. It also protects the plant against intruders, such as virus particles and bacteria.

Flowering plants

A summer field is a riot of brilliant yellows. Black-eyed Susans, goldenrod, honeysuckle, and evening primrose splash bright yellows against the green stems and leaves. The bright colours attract bees, birds, beetles, and butterflies. Those animals drink the flower nectar and help the plants **reproduce**.

Flowering plants are called **angiosperms**. The word angiosperm comes from the Greek words *angion* (container) and *sperma* (seed). In simple terms, angiosperms are seed containers. Angiosperms include the flowers, fruits, and vegetables in your garden. They have roots, stems, and leaves. <u>Flowering parent plants produce young plants by seeds.</u>

TINY FLOWER ALERT!

Wolffia plants produce the smallest flowers in the world. A dozen wolffia flowers will fit on the head of a pin.

Ladybirds and some types of wasps help pollinate yellow flowers.

A variety of flowers

Flowers come in many shapes and sizes. They can be as large as an open umbrella or smaller than the point of a pin. They come in colours ranging from white to deep purple, and all the yellows, blues, pinks, reds, greens, and oranges in between. Some flowers bloom for weeks, while others, like the night-blooming cereus, only open one night a year. Some flowers smell beautiful, while others smell like rotting flesh. The sizes, shapes, colours, and scents of flowers have only one purpose: to help the plants reproduce.

Parts of a flower

The flower is where **reproduction** occurs in a plant. Flower parts include **pollen** and **ovules**, which are the sperm and eggs of a plant. <u>For reproduction to occur, the pollen (sperm) must **fertilize** the ovules (eggs)</u>. When that occurs, the flower begins to develop seeds.

STIGMA
The sticky part of the carpel that collects pollen

STYLE
The tube-like part of the carpel that connects the stigma to the ovary

SEPAL
Leaf-like plant parts that protect a flower bud before it opens

RECEPTACLE
The top of a stem that holds the flower

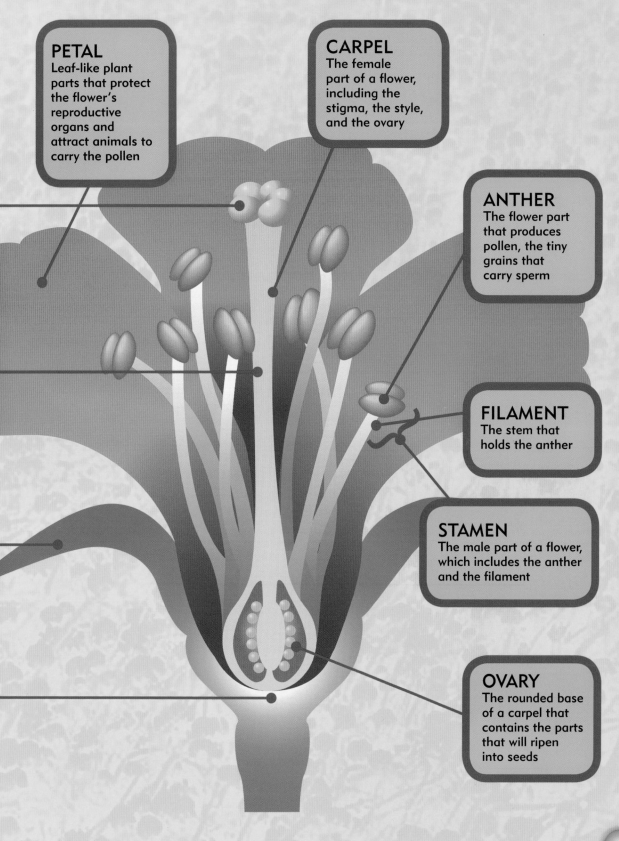

PETAL
Leaf-like plant parts that protect the flower's reproductive organs and attract animals to carry the pollen

CARPEL
The female part of a flower, including the stigma, the style, and the ovary

ANTHER
The flower part that produces pollen, the tiny grains that carry sperm

FILAMENT
The stem that holds the anther

STAMEN
The male part of a flower, which includes the anther and the filament

OVARY
The rounded base of a carpel that contains the parts that will ripen into seeds

POLLINATION

It is springtime, you breathe in and sneeze. It is possible you have an allergy to **pollen**. When flowers bloom, their pollen fills the air. Although pollen may be annoying, it is an important part of plant life. Without pollen, there would be no apples or bananas, no corn or broccoli, and absolutely no chocolate.

Pollen

Pollen is the male cells, or sperm, of a plant. A flowering plant produces pollen on the **anthers**, the male organs of flowers. The pollen needs to be transferred from the anthers to the **stigma**, the female part of a flower. <u>The act of transferring pollen is called **pollination**</u>. Pollen **fertilizes** flowers so plants can produce grain, fruit, nuts, and vegetables.

Pollen can be carried on the air every time the wind blows. It can also be transferred by water, either by rain or in streams and rivers. The most common way to transfer pollen is with the help of animals. Animals, especially insects, pollinate nine out of ten flower species.

Types of flowers	Most common animal pollinators
Fruit trees, vegetable plants	Bees, beetles, butterflies
Night-blooming flowers, cactus	Bats, moths, hummingbirds
Tropical flowers	Bees, flies
Tropical flowering trees	Lemurs, bats, Australian possums, geckos

Honeybees and humans

Honeybees are very important pollinators. They seek flowers in search of nectar so they can make honey. Their fuzzy bodies rub against pollen. The bees drink the nectar and fly away. When they leave the flower, they take pollen with them. A bee will visit many flowers on a fruit tree or in a field. Each visit deposits pollen collected earlier in the day and picks up new pollen to take on the next flight.

Sometimes humans pollinate plants. They do this to create new species of plants. When humans pollinate plants for this reason, the process is called **crossbreeding**.

Each year, bees around the world pollinate fruit and vegetable crops.

Bat pollinators

Darkness comes to the desert, and cacti open their blooms to their midnight visitors. The white blooms are large – 2.5 to 8 centimetres (1 to 3.5 inches) – across, so that bats can see them. They have ample amounts of nectar for the bats to drink, and plenty of pollen for their visitors to carry away. Cacti are not the only plants that depend on bats. Nearly 300 species of fruit rely on bats to carry their pollen.

Foul-smelling flower!

A rafflesia bud grows into an enormous, foul-smelling flower, measuring up to 90 centimetres (3 feet) in diameter. The flower's perfume smells like rotting meat so it will attract flies. The flies flock to the flower to lay their maggots. As they do so, they take pollen away from the rafflesia. In the Indonesian rainforests, the flies then pollinate other rafflesia plants.

SCIENCE IN ACTION

POLLEN THROUGH A MICROSCOPE

What you need:

- ☑ a needle
- ☑ a flower (a lily works well)
- ☑ a glass slide
- ☑ a microscope

What you do:

- Using the eye end of a needle, remove pollen from a flower.
- Place the pollen on a slide and view it through a microscope.
- Draw what you see through the microscope.

Seeds

The average kitchen cupboard is full of seeds, such as walnuts, almonds, and peanuts. A grain of rice is a type of grass seed. Flour is ground up wheat seeds, and coffee comes from roasted, ground beans. Pinto beans, lentils, and corn are seeds we put in chilli, soup, and salads. We even squash seeds to make oil from corn and soybeans.

From baby to adult

A seed is an **embryo**, or a baby plant. Seeds form after a plant is fertilized with **pollen**. A seed has three basic parts. The outside is the seed coat. It protects the seed from drying out or from damage when the seed drops from the plant. Inside the seed is a young plant, called a **sporophyte**. Given water and sun, the young plant will grow roots and a stem. The third part of a seed is the stored food. This food nourishes the baby plant as it grows. The period when a baby plant begins to grow into an adult plant and breaks out of its coating is called **germination.**

Gigantic seeds!

The largest seeds in the world grow on the coco-de-mer palm. Found in the Seychelles Islands in the Indian Ocean, these huge seeds can measure 30 centimetres (12 inches) long and 90 centimetres (3 feet) wide. Each seed can weigh up to 18 kilograms (40 pounds). Yes, a coconut is a seed!

Millennium Seed Bank

The Millennium Seed Bank is helping to save endangered plants throughout the world. Scientists think there may be 60,000 to 100,000 plant species that may disappear from our world. The Seed Bank collects and stores seeds from plants believed to be extinct in the wild. To date, the Seed Bank had preserved seeds from 20,495 species of endangered plants. Based in Kew Gardens in London, the Seed Bank works with organizations in the United States, Mexico, Australia, Botswana, Burkina Faso, Chile, China, Jordan, Kenya, Lebanon, Madagascar, Malawi, Mali, Namibia, South Africa, and Tanzania.

Many seeds have a hard outer coating that cracks open for the seed to sprout. The roots grow down to draw up water.

Plants on the Moon

If humans ever set up a colony on the Moon, they will need to grow their own food. In 2007 and 2008, NASA began the NASA Engineering Design Challenge: Lunar Plant Growth Chamber Project to work out just how that will happen. Students of all age groups were asked to design, build, and evaluate containers for growing plants in space. Teachers could request cinnamon basil seeds that had flown on the STS-118 space shuttle mission from NASA. Wouldn't it be exciting to create a way to grow carrots on the Moon?

ANCIENT SEEDS

Seeds can lie inactive for centuries. In June 2005, scientists found seeds from a date palm at King Herod's Palace near the Dead Sea. The seeds were about 2,000 years old. Given water, sun, and a place to grow, one of the seeds produced a healthy palm sprout.

The world's record for the oldest seed is from an Arctic lupine. The seed was dug up from a lemming burrow in frozen Arctic tundra. It germinated and flowered after being inactive for 10,000 years!

Dates, shown in the picture to the left, and coconuts are two types of palm tree seeds.

SCIENCE IN ACTION

A CLOSER LOOK AT BEANS

What you need:

 7 dried pinto beans

 a ruler

 ½ cup of water

What you do:

- Measure and record the sizes of 7 dried pinto beans.

- Soak the beans in ½ cup of water overnight.

- Measure the beans again. What do you find? Look at the skin on the beans. How has it changed?

- Gently remove the skin and open the bean. What do you see?

Seed diSpersal

Take a walk through any meadow. Afterwards, you will probably find small seeds stuck to your socks, shoes, and jeans. If you observed those seeds under a microscope, you would see tiny hooks. Those seeds depend on animals that pass by to carry them to a new home.

Have you ever found small dandelion seeds stuck to your clothes?

Water, wind, or animals

It would be useless for a plant to produce seeds that stay within centimetres of the parent plant. One small area can only support a limited number of plants. The soil, **nutrients**, water, and sunlight available in any one spot is limited. Spreading seeds far and wide increases the opportunity for the seeds to take root and grow. <u>The act of spreading seeds is called seed **dispersal**.</u>

Plants can spread their seeds in water, on wind, or with the help of animals. When rain falls on a forest, the runoff water can carry seeds and deposit them far away from the parent plant. The seeds could end up in a stream and may even take a longer journey. Seeds, such as those on dandelions, dry up and blow away in the wind. Other seeds have burrs that catch on the fur of animals as they pass. Whichever way a seed travels, its trip is a necessary part of the plant life cycle.

POP!
Gorse seeds burst out with a POP! that can be heard many metres away. When the seedpod explodes, the action hurls the seeds away from the parent plant.

ANIMAL DUNG

Animals eat plants and fruit then pass the seeds along in their dung. Most seeds have hard coverings to protect them. Many of these seeds are not digested in an animal's body. Even animals that specifically eat seeds do not digest all the seeds they eat. Some seeds pass out of the animal with other body waste. This is a successful means of seed dispersal. The dung provides water, heat, and fertilizer – three elements needed for seeds to grow.

CREATING NEW PLANT SPECIES

In the 1800s, an Austrian monk named Gregor Mendel studied how offspring inherited characteristics from parents. Mendel did his work with sweet peas. Some **genes**, said Mendel, were **dominant**. Dominant genes were stronger than other genes. Mendel called the weaker genes **recessive** genes.

According to Mendel, it would be possible to predict the characteristics of plants if you knew the dominant or stronger characteristics. Using this idea, **botanists** have developed stronger, more productive fruit, vegetable, and grain **hybrids**.

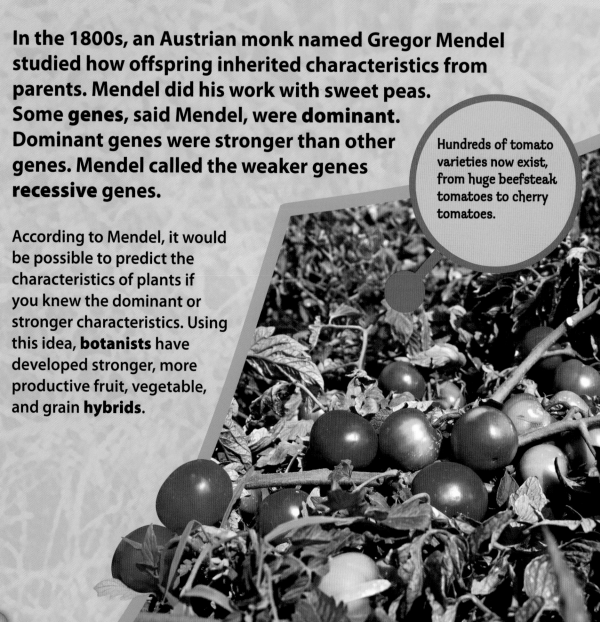

Hundreds of tomato varieties now exist, from huge beefsteak tomatoes to cherry tomatoes.

Punnett squares

Punnett squares are used to show the likely results of **crossbreeding** plants or animals. For example, a scientist is trying to create a totally seedless cucumber. Heavy seed genes are dominant and are marked S. Low seed genes are recessive and marked s. The scientist crossbreeds two cucumber species that carry recessive, low-seed genes (Ss). The punnett square shows that one out of four cucumber plants should have only the recessive genes (ss). That means, if the scientist continues to breed the ss cucumbers, the result should eventually be seedless cucumbers.

	S	s
S	SS	Ss
s	Ss	ss

Hybrid species

Scientists develop new hybrid species by crossbreeding different varieties of the same plant. They might try to make the new plant species better able to resist disease. They might want a higher crop yield or prettier flowers. Among the hybrid products that people enjoy are varieties of roses, seedless cucumbers, seedless grapefruit, nectarines, and sweet onions.

WOW!

Eight hundred years ago, the Incas of Peru developed more than 200 species of potatoes by crossbreeding. They bred potatoes that could be grown at high altitudes or with little water or in poor soil. All the potatoes that are eaten today are related in some way to the Inca potato species Solanum Tuberosa.

SCIENCE IN ACTION

PREDICT THE TRAITS OF NEW PLANTS

You are crossbreeding two hybrids of corn. One hybrid has large kernels (Kk). The other hybrid has small kernels (kk). After breeding, what is the chance of getting small kernel corn from this breeding experiment?

What you need:

 paper and pencil

What you do:

- Draw a punnett square.

- Following the model on page 25, enter the genetic codes for kernels (Kk and kk).

- Predict the varieties of corn that will come from mixing the two corn varieties.

Norman Borlaug: Botanist

In 1970 American botanist Norman Borlaug won the Nobel Peace Prize. This is an unusual prize for an agricultural scientist to win. Borlaug won because he developed a wheat hybrid with a short stalk, low water usage, and high grain yield. Borlaug's short stalk wheat is ideal for feeding people in drought-stricken countries, such as Pakistan, India, and Mexico. His wheat helps feed millions of hungry people.

CLONES, RUNNERS, AND BULBS

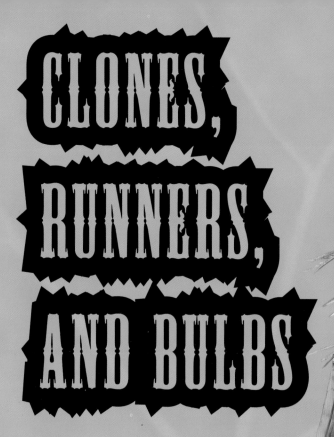

You plant a small patch of bamboo in the garden. The following year, you have twice as much bamboo. Five years later, bamboo is popping up all over the garden. How does this happen? The bamboo roots sent **rhizomes** underground. The new plants sprout from that original, small bamboo patch.

New bamboo plants sprout when other bamboo plants send rhizomes underground.

Asexual reproduction

This type of **reproduction** is called **vegetative** reproduction, or **asexual** reproduction. <u>**Vegetative reproduction does not require sperm or eggs.**</u> It depends on the parent plant growing new plants through its stems, roots, or leaves. The new plants are called daughter plants or **daughter colonies**. The parent plant makes an identical **clone** of itself. Here are the ways that different types of plants reproduce by forms of asexual reproduction:

Piggyback plants
Plantlets

Some plants produce buds along the edges or at the base of their leaves. The buds develop into tiny plants called **plantlets**. Piggyback plants produce new plants this way. Eventually, the plantlets fall away from the parent plant. They send down roots into the soil and grow to become separate plants that can create new plantlets.

Lilacs
Root sprouts and suckers

Some plants have roots that sprout a new plant. Lilacs and crepe myrtles develop new plants through root sprouts or suckers. These plants grow fast, and a single sprout quickly produces a thick patch of plants.

Grape vines
Cuttings

Many plants can make a new plant from a piece that has broken or been cut off. Ivy, grape vines, and blackberry plants can grow from cuttings. This does not mean any dropped leaf will produce a new plant. The cutting must be a stem with plant **nodes**. The cutting is placed in water or damp soil and roots sprout.

Science in the kitchen

Take cuttings from several different plants, such as ivy, geraniums, and coleus. Make sure you cut the branch on an angle. Place each cutting in a separate jar of water with a small amount (10 grams or 1/4 teaspoon) of plant fertilizer. More than half the plant must be above the water line. When roots grow and reach about 5 to 7 centimetres (2 to 3 inches) long, plant the cutting in soil.

Strawberries

Runners

Runners are stems that grow along the ground. A runner breaks off from a node and travels along the ground. Strawberries and spider plants produce new plants by using runners. The runner sends roots down to get water and **nutrients** from the soil. Where a node appears, a new plant will begin to develop. Eventually, the runner stem dies off leaving the new plant to continue growing.

Aspen trees

Clones

Aspen trees create new trees by cloning. One tree can reproduce itself thousands of times. Each clone carries the identical **DNA** or genetic make-up of its parents. In the Wasatch Mountains of Utah, one aspen tree has cloned itself 47,000 times. That is a stand of genetically identical aspen trees. The entire stand is called a clone. The clone has developed by sending suckers from one gigantic root system. The aboveground trees appear to be separate plants, but they are not. The aspen clone is one massive plant with a huge root system.

Grass

Rhizomes

Rhizomes are stems that grow horizontally below the ground. Grass, asparagus, and irises use rhizomes to produce new plants. Rhizomes have buds instead of nodes. The buds grow and send new shoots and roots up from the rhizomes.

Potatoes

Tubers

Tubers are the large swollen tips of a rhizome stem. Potatoes and yams are tubers. A potato has buds on its surface and these buds are often called "eyes". Each bud can produce new shoots and roots, so one potato can produce more than one new plant.

Tulips

Bulbs

Bulbs are another type of underground stem. Onions and tulips are bulbs. The stem is found at the bottom of bulbs and it is in the shape of a disc. Roots grow down from this stem disc, while shoots grow up from the tip of the bulb.

Science in the kitchen

Let a potato sit in a cool place until it grows "eyes". Cut the potato into sections, each section having an eye. Plant each potato section in soil in a large pot. Place the pot in a sunny spot. Water only enough to keep the soil damp.

Eventually flowers will bloom on the plants. This is a signal that tubers are beginning to develop. When the plant above the ground dies, the potatoes are ready to dig up. Potatoes can be kept for several months in a cool, dark, dry place.

Conifers

A pine cone drops to the floor of the forest; it rolls down a slope and falls into a stream. The pine cone floats and is carried downstream, far away, where it finally comes to rest and releases its seeds. With luck, one of the seeds will produce a new pine tree.

Conifer trees produce pine cones. These are plants that produce seeds, but do not grow flowers. Plants in this group include pines, firs, cedars, and spruces. They also include ginkgos, cycads (certain palm trees), and some shrubs.

Scientists call plants like pines **gymnosperms**. The word gymnosperm comes from the Greek words *gymnos* (naked) and *sperma* (seed). Gymnosperms are plants that have naked seeds. These seeds have no coating and can be eaten and digested by animals. An animal may take the cone back to its home habitat, sprinkling seeds from the cone along the way.

Life cycle of a pine

A seed from a pine grows into a mature tree after several years. The adult pine develops two types of cone: male and female. The male cones produce **pollen** that contains sperm. The female cones produce eggs. Wind carries the pollen to the female cones and **fertilizes** the eggs. The fertilized eggs are in a pine cone. The eggs develop into seeds. When the cone drops, it releases the seeds. Under the right conditions, the seeds will produce young pine trees.

Fire!

Lightning strikes and brings fire to the forest. A natural fire, such as this one, may be a good thing. Fire destroys standing trees and plant matter on the forest floor, but it also renews the forest. For many pine species, fire gives life.

The ashes left after a forest fire return **nutrients** to the soil. The pine seeds find a healthy environment in which to grow. With sun, water, and rich soil, new pine trees grow from the seeds released by the fire. These are the resources a plant needs to grow strong and healthy. Fire has brought new life to the pine forest.

Lodgepole pines and many other pines produce cones that do not easily release their seeds. Only a forest fire produces enough heat to make the cones open.

A glue-like resin coats many pine cones and seals the cone. The heat from a forest fire melts the resin. The cone is no longer held closed, and it can release its seeds.

Preventing forest fires

Although forest fires can benefit some plant species, they are very dangerous for animals and humans. Deliberately starting a forest fire is a crime called arson and is against the law. Never play with matches or campfires. Leave the work of fire to Mother Nature. You can and should prevent forest fires.

SCIENCE IN ACTION

STUDYING PINE CONES

What you need:

 several sheets of newspaper

 2 rags about 15 x 15 cm (6 x 6 in)

 immature pine cones with closed scales

 a bowl with warm water

 tweezers

What you do:

• Soak the pine cones in water for about 2 hours. Remove from the water and dry the cones.

• Spread newspaper on a table to protect the surface.

• Wrap one rag around each end of a pine cone.

• Holding tightly, twist the pine cone until the scales open.

• Shake the cones to release the seeds. If the seeds do not come out easily, use the tweezers to pull them out. How many seeds did you find in each cone? Did you predict that, in a forest, each seed becomes a mature pine tree? Why or why not? What resources do you think a pine seed needs to become a tree? What might prevent a seed from growing?

REPRODUCTION BY SPORES

A giant European puffball begins to swell, and the outer wall of the puffball becomes hard. One touch is all it needs, and POOF! The puffball bursts and millions of tiny spores burst out like a puff of smoke.

Not all plants **reproduce** with seeds. Some, such as ferns and mosses, reproduce using spores. Like seeds, spores are tiny plant embryos. Plants that reproduce using spores can be either **non-vascular** plants (mosses, liverworts, and hornworts) or **vascular** plants (ferns and horsetails). Fungi – mushrooms and toadstools – also reproduce using spores.

The puff of smoke to the right is actually tiny spores exploding from a puffball!

Life cycle of a fern

Ferns grow in many places, from the chilly Arctic tundra to tropical rainforests. Some species are extremely small, while others grow into trees that reach more than 20 metres (66 feet) high. Ferns have lacy leaves that may look a bit like feathers. Ferns, horsetails, and club mosses are vascular plants that reproduce through spores.

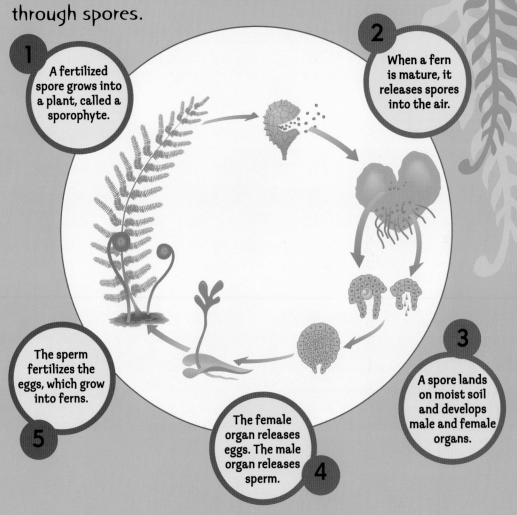

1 A fertilized spore grows into a plant, called a sporophyte.

2 When a fern is mature, it releases spores into the air.

3 A spore lands on moist soil and develops male and female organs.

4 The female organ releases eggs. The male organ releases sperm.

5 The sperm fertilizes the eggs, which grow into ferns.

Fungi

You come into contact with fungi every day. Yeast is a fungus that makes bread rise. Mushrooms in your food are also fungus. Fungi are unusual plants. Unlike green plants, fungi cannot make their own food. They cannot catch food, either. Instead, they absorb food. Many fungi thrive on dead plants or animal matter. Some experts estimate that there may be as many as 1.5 million different fungus species. Only 100,000 of these species have been identified.

Fungi, like ferns, reproduce through spores. The difference between fungi and ferns, however, is that fungi usually produce huge numbers of spores. One giant puffball, for example, may shoot 7 trillion spores into the air. Very few of these spores turn into new puffballs.

How do you think these fungi reproduce? The answer is to your left!

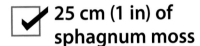

SCIENCE IN ACTION

SPHAGNUM MOSS

What you need:

- ☑ 25 cm (1 in) of sphagnum moss
- ☑ a cup filled with water
- ☑ scales that measure grams

What you do:

- Weigh the piece of moss and record the weight.

- Place the moss in the cup of water.

- Let it soak for 15 minutes.

- Carefully remove the moss and shake off the excess water. What do you notice about the moss? Weigh the moss. How much **mass** did the moss gain? What does this show you about moss?

- You might discover this fascinating fact about sphagnum moss (also called peat moss): it can hold up to 20 times its dry weight in water in its cells!

Timeline

425 million years ago

Early land plants leave microscopic fossils behind.

9000 BCE

Barley and oat seeds from this time period are found in the Jordan Valley. This tells us that people were cultivating crops in this region about 11,000 years ago.

2760 BCE

The oldest bristlecone pine tree surviving today begins to grow.

1863

Mendel experiments with developing new sweet pea hybrids.

1500

Beans, lima beans, and sweet potatoes are introduced to Europe from North America.

1871

Luther Burbank develops the russet Burbank potato. This is a hybrid potato produced by crossbreeding and is the most popular baking potato in North America.

1970

Norman Borlaug wins the Nobel Peace Prize for developing short-stalk wheat.

50,000 BCE

Early people leave wild date seeds in the Shanidar Cave, Iraq. The people saved the seeds to plant crops they needed to survive.

200 BCE

0

773 CE

The oldest redwood tree surviving today in North America begins to grow. That tree is over 2,200 years old!

The French emperor Charlemagne orders grape cuttings to be planted in France.

1492

1200

Columbus returns to Europe from the West Indies with many new plants, including corn.

Incas in Peru begin developing varieties of potato.

1982

1990

2006

NOW

The first genetically-engineered crop is grown by scientists at Washington University in Missouri, USA. Genetic engineering means that botanists developed the species of plant in their laboratory and grew it as a crop.

Project SEEDS was launched by NASA and The George W. Park Seed Co., allowing students across the United States to compare growth of seeds exposed to conditions of space with that of seeds stored on Earth.

The Millennium Seed Bank based in Kew in London contains seeds from 20,495 species and the collection is still growing.

Plant quiz

1 Pollen contains
a) plant sperm   b) plant eggs
c) dust   d) seeds

2 The most common means of pollination is by
a) wind   b) bats
c) water   d) insects

3 Some pine cones cannot release their seeds unless they
a) are exposed to a forest fire.
b) lie on the forest floor for a year.
c) are buried in moist soil.
d) come in contact with a running stream.

4 You can produce a clone of a parent plant if you
a) grow a plant from an old seed
b) grow a new plant from a cutting
c) pollinate a pine cone
d) crossbreed two species of corn

5 The female part of a flower is the
a) receptacle
b) carpel
c) petal
d) sepal

6 A plant that can reproduce by sending runners above the soil is
a) a potato   b) a lilac bush
c) a strawberry   d) grass

7 Ferns reproduce through
a) pine cones
b) seeds
c) roots and sprouts
d) spores

8 The part of a flower that produces pollen is
a) the ovary   b) the anther
c) the sepal   d) the seeds

9 Plants that transport water and food through their systems are called
a) vascular plants
b) seedless plants
c) non-vascular plants
d) fungi

10 Which part of a flowering plant is important for reproduction?
a) the cuticle
b) the roots
c) the leaves
d) the flower

Glossary

algae marine plant with no leaves, roots, or stems, for example seaweed and kelp

angiosperm flowering plant that reproduces through seeds

anther male organ of a flowering plant that produces pollen

asexual not involving male or female sexual organs

bacteria unicellular organisms found in every habitat on Earth; bacteria can be the cause of many diseases

botanist scientist who studies plants

bulb type of undergound stem, for example tulips and onions

carpel female reproductive organs of a flower

clone exact genetic copy

conifer plant that produces seeds in cones

crossbreed taking two different breeds or species of plant and "crossing" them to create a hybrid or species

cuticle waxy covering on the leaves and stem of a plant

daughter colony group of plants cloned from a parent plant

dispersal distribution or spreading, as in seeds

DNA (deoxyribonucleic acid) molecule that carries the genetic code

dominant having the greatest power or control

embryo developing young of a species

fertilize to unite a female egg with a male sperm to produce offspring

filament tube that holds up the anther

genes substance that carries characteristics like flower colour and leaf shape from parents to their offspring

germination act of growing a plant from a seed

gymnosperm non-flowering plant that reproduces through seeds

hybrid plant species made from crossbreeding two other plants

lichen plant that is a blend of algae and fungi

mass amount of matter something contains

node knob, bud, or swelling on a stem or branch

non-vascular describes a plant that has no internal system for transporting water or food

nutrient substance in food that plants and animals need in order to function

organism living thing

ovary female organ that holds eggs

ovule small or immature eggs that develop into seeds after fertilization

plantlets tiny plants

pollen powdery substance of flowering plants that contains sperm

pollination act of carrying pollen from one flower of a species to another flower of the same species

pollution act of damaging air, water, or soil with chemicals

receptacle end of a plant stem that holds a flower

recessive having less power or control

reproduction act of producing young

rhizome thick underground horizontal stem that produces roots and shoots, such as in grass

runner stem that grows along the ground; it breaks off from the node and travels along the top of the ground

sepal protective structure that surrounds a flower bud

sporophyte plant that grows from spores or a young plant

stamen male reproductive organs that consist of an anther and a filament

stigma sticky pad on a flower that collects pollen

style tube-like stem that connects the stigma and the ovary of a flower

tuber large, swollen tip of a rhizome stem; an example of a tuber is a potato

vascular describes a plant that has a system to transport water and food

vegetative process of reproduction that does not include seeds or spores

Further information

Books

Eyewitness Guide: Plants, David Burnie (Dorling Kindersley, 2003)

Plant Cells: The Building Blocks of Plants, Darlene R. Stille Compass Point Books, 2006)

Plant Parts, Louise and Richard Spilsbury (Heinemann Library, 2008)

Plant Reproduction, Louise and Richard Spilsbury (Heinemann Library, 2008)

The Plant Life Cycle, Cheryl Jakab (Smart Apple Media, 2007)

Websites

www.kew.org/msbp/index.htm
This website explains all about the Millennium Seed Bank project based at Kew in London.

www.countrysideinfo.co.uk/flplcont.htm
Have a look at the site of the Offwell Woodland and Wildlife Trust. Find out how flowering plants disperse their seeds.

www.countrysideinfo.co.uk/lifecycles/lifecyc1.htm
This webpage presents a general plant life cycle.

www.bbc.co.uk/schools/ks2bitesize/science/revision_bites/life_cycles. shtml
This website focuses on plant life cycles and plant parts.

Disclaimer
All the Internet addresses (URLs) given in this book were valid at the time of going to press. However, due to the dynamic nature of the Internet, some addresses may have changed, or sites may have ceased to exist since publication. While the author and publishers regret any inconvenience this may cause readers, no responsibility for any such changes can be accepted by either the author or the publishers.

Index